The Hidden Wilderness

poems by

Linda Ann Suddarth

Finishing Line Press
Georgetown, Kentucky

The Hidden Wilderness

Copyright © 2019 by Linda Ann Suddarth
ISBN 978-1-63534-880-4 First Edition
All rights reserved under International and Pan-American Copyright Conventions. No part of this book may be reproduced in any manner whatsoever without written permission from the publisher, except in the case of brief quotations embodied in critical articles and reviews.

ACKNOWLEDGMENTS

"A Local Habitation and a Name," appeared in *Anima*, Summer 2015
"Curious and Rich," appeared in *Parabola*, Summer 2014. (web)
"Spring for Edwin," appeared in *Parabola*, Fall 2011
"Insufficient Funds," appeared in *Hudson View*, Spring 2009
"Happy Other-Place," "Borrowed Forest, Rented Thicket," and "Curious and Rich," appeared in *Mythopoetry*, Spring 2017
"The White Curtain," and "Moonlight Found Me," appeared in the Micro-Chap, *Wandering Barefoot, OrigamiPoems*. Spring 2018

Publisher: Leah Maines
Editor: Christen Kincaid
Cover Art: Linda Ann Suddarth
Author Photo: Lydia Greer, https://www.lydiagreer.com
Cover Design: Leah Huete

Printed in the USA on acid-free paper.
Order online: www.finishinglinepress.com
        also available on amazon.com

Author inquiries and mail orders:
Finishing Line Press
P. O. Box 1626
Georgetown, Kentucky 40324
U. S. A.

Table of Contents

Curious and Rich 1

Happy Other-Place 2

Musical Scores 3

Me of Cloud and Sea 4

White on White 5

Where to Leave You 6

Borrowed Forest, Rented Thicket 8

Clouds are Angels 10

Born to Earth: Newgrange 11

A Local Habitation and a Name 13

Winter Morning 15

The Sky is My Monastery, the Forest My Cathedral 16

Insufficient Funds 18

Spring for Edwin 19

Dramas at Work 21

Salutations from the Sea 22

The White Curtain 23

Moonlight Found Me 24

Light Shining Through Purple Glass 25

*For Lydia Katherine Greer, Rachel Elizabeth Greer,
and Loretta Greer Jean*

Curious and Rich

When I walk past
the fragrant forest
after heavy rain,
which smells like
the freshest salad
you ever ate,
some vegetation
from Otherworld
that when eaten
makes you feel alive,

then I listen, listen
and there is
nothing, nothing but.

When it is almost dusk
and the horizon is tinged
with the most delicate
hint of lavender,
against it dark
silhouettes of tiny
fruit-tree branches,

I listen, listen
there is nothing, nothing but.

When I pass the small mountain
rising like a god
impressing the night
and the still liquid sky,

I listen, listen
and there is nothing, nothing.

But nothing is something
curious and rich,
and I have heard it.

Happy Other-Place

With every rain the woods
grow another foot,
on the breeze
rose and honeysuckle
faintly permeate
the corners of the sky.
In the far-seeing
of distance is
the blue of mountain
through the tree tops:
the mountain that looks
down on all of us.
I've been there,
these are the apple groves
up on top of the blue.
One fall we sat
under an apple tree,
spread a blanket
and ate apple pie,
while the bees
resembled angels
singing all in harmony.
People strolled in a daze
with apple nets
in their hands,
collecting the harvest
in this happy
other-place.

Musical Scores

A thousand tiny animals
shake a thousand tiny rattles
in the woods, in the moonlight
all night long.
In the day
a thousand different tiny animals
shake a thousand different ratchets,
the scores that play
behind this story
of summer sleeping
and summer waking.

Me of Cloud and Sea *

Sometimes the *me*
comes spilling over,
I can't hold
the pink tops
of giant cumulous,
rising from tall
secret-filled evergreen,
that have ridden
on the stormy wind,
from crashing,
foaming, roaring
me of sea forever.

*The italic *me* is from the Sumerian poem of Inanna

White on White

There's a full moon today
but I won't be able to see it,
this day is full of snow.
Falling, floating, powder:
a cloud of cover
over the body of my earth.
All day we can fall
into her beautiful, lacy
pillows until
all the lovely
piles up delicious.
Sugary kissed tree-limbs
bury us in some
enchantment far far
away from anyone.
We are each other's igloo
be here white on white
finally, finally, surrender
and roll ourselves in sugar,
as if the winter world
were warm inside us,
coconut cake just from the oven.
Kisses from heaven
cascade down all day.
We continue to drift,
dance to the earth
and pile up sweetly.

Where to Leave You

My little daughters
said goodbye
to their imaginary friends
at the Metropolitan
Museum of Art.
They chose for the friends
to live in the French
Decorative period:
they had beautiful furniture
and a guard at the door.
They said goodbye,
that they'd come back
for a visit
every now and then,
but we didn't.
Life became too honest
too full to always
have someone around
who was invisible.
So it is with you.
I must be honest
because, to speak, to act
is to grasp time:
your presence is
too much to ask.
No more innuendos
no more wrapping
my heart with
the ending of your poem.
I will leave you to live
in a pretty world
richly furnished,

maybe the Rotunda Dome,
in Charlottesville
with its perfect beauty
and symmetry,
I leave you
in a sacred space.

Borrowed Forest, Rented Thicket

My comfort falls on deaf ears.
Though you are only volunteers,
comical encroaching
forest with your odd smells:
sweet, tangy mid-spring,
hints of honeysuckle, cedar,
thyme, vinegar, rose, float,
don't you know tomorrow
will be the back-hoe,
saws, bulldozers,
and your lovely thickets
will be undone?
Strange tiny flowers, like bells
and purple prehistoric shaped,
beside the poke berry
monster, decorated
with pieces of old fence.
You're not sad?
Little birds, find other nests.
Yesterday when the crow
sat eating your young
on the telephone wire,
stolen from you,
and from the maple,
didn't you see
that was a sign to scatter?
Yet you still sing,
sitting in the tree
that will be gone tomorrow.
The maple who has given
much shade and color
isn't sad either. She
is giving me strength.
In my heart,
borrowed forest, rented thicket,

you are forever,
many and varied shades of green,
and ever joyous in your singing.
Someday I'll put some money
down and buy some wild place:
let it be what it is.

Clouds are Angels

Clouds are angels now,
changing as they float
across the sky.
All summer was
Corot and Monet.
But now with leaves golden
the landscape becomes Rubens
scarlet and gold,
giant pink cotton candy
like baby-butts,
towering above the
tastefulness of an
old Virginia town.
Angels, constant, are present
talking, almost babbling
there is so much to say.
Something is happening,
as a cool breeze strikes up
bend towards me.
Know many invisibles
are now present,
otherworld resides
alongside concerns
with paying the bills
and washing the dishes.
One only needs
to see, to listen
to background sounds.
Angels are tiny insects
singing in the trees,
and bubbling river
flowing to the sea
in pure joy,
about to split her seams.

Born to the Earth: Newgrange

They move all around
glimpsed by feeling
in the greenness of moss
in the otherworld wind
that blows a deep silence
atop an ancient hill.
In the passage to the
womb of the earth
I am being born
this time, as I go in,
not as I come out.
Born to the earth
rather than the air.
This zipping into other
time and space
is easy, yet
I am stunned
something has just
happened to me,
will I ever fully
grasp what?
The ground sways
back and forth.
it's not the ground
of the new world.
I will take this
hand-branch of the tree
and what it knows
it will pass onto me—
as the otherworld wind
blows, the dusk settles
and a farmer and dog
gather in the lambs.
They have been
scattered on the hill of Tara
where ancient kings married
the goddess—the earth—all one.

Writing this in the hills
of Virginia, I look up
and see four little deer
run through the winter woods.
At once, I am here in magic,
and I am there in magic,
as thresholds to
other worlds
make their appearance
in every place.
Even one tree alongside
a superhighway
can beckon to me,
perhaps this is what
it means to be
born to the earth.

A Local Habitation and a Name

To sit in the moonlight
wrapped in a blanket
rocking back and forth.

As the dark grows
I hear many walking
in the woods
I see only shadows
in the pale light
as they walk or
scramble through the
fallen leaves.

I hear breathing,
some walk slowly
stopping to consider,
others follow each other
in a mad dash,
all the while
the owl hoots
high up in his overview.

Nocturnal comings
and goings,
dreams while awake,
bathing in cold moonlight
all heals an un-named pain.

Beauty, movement, animal
beings, dream sequences,
happen outside me now.

The dark formless
inner stirrings
take shape
and are given
"a local habitation
and a name."*

* from William Shakespeare's *A Midsummer Night's Dream*

Winter Morning

The trees held strong
tall and truly themselves
in the windy night.
Old white oak didn't
fall on the house,
didn't quit its job
of over-seeing
of covering over.
This winter morning
surprises in stillness
a soft golden light
falling on sweet
warriors poised
with naked beautiful
limbs still
but always ready
for dance.

The Sky Is My Monastery, the Forest My Cathedral

The sky is my monastery
the forest my cathedral
and so I must constantly
go to church
to seek,
throughout the world
all the places
of sublime beauty,
and like them
must mimic
divine light
not doing anything
but just be
who I am.

This is a new time
and I no longer need
to be a sacrifice
labeled a virgin, or a whore,
burned at the stake,
thrown into prison,
or over the wall
of Edinburgh castle
into the North Sea.
That's over.

I am healed
and not afraid
to be me and free
from religion and politics
and misogyny.
I can heal you too
by just being me.
though to speak it
sounds crazy.

No words then
I will mimic divine light
and just be,
with the forest as cathedral,
and the sky as monastery.

Insufficient Funds

People can die of
a broken heart
you know.

I can't afford
that look on your face.

There isn't enough
in my piggy-bank
saved up for you.

Don't hold me
that close,
I forgot where I hid
the cash under the mattress.

Don't say things like that:
a foolish girl
closed the books
on this one
a long time ago.

She got
carried away,
and spent
oh so much
all on one
investment.

Spring for Edwin

I went out to meet
the wind half-way;
something new is always
turning up,
though the crows complain.

When Mom died
Daddy went to the ocean
to meet the tossing
the change halfway.

It should be winter
longer than this.
For a very long time
I should be buried
in snow.

It seems wrong
that the very day
you were buried
change should ripple
out in such a way.

Everything blooms in shock.

The spring equinox has come
and someone else will
be the teller of the seasons
since you are strangely silent.

Yet the master of language
you are, now speaks
in perfect metaphor—wind,
the red-bud tree, the deer
in the back yard.

You continue,
evenso,
my heart is in some
snowy place.

Dramas at Work

There is a man
who dreams of me
or two or three men,
who dream of me.
I too do the dance
of the unavailable.
In dream
we tickle each other
with our toes.
We, all caught up
in what we cannot have
what we think
we cannot be.
We, all caught up
in who we are not.

There is a woman
who has nightmares of me
or two or three women
who have nightmares of me.
It's not that I am
too honest, though
known to be,
but that kindness falls
on the floor between us.
No one has been kind,
and it smells suspicious.
We, all caught up
in what we cannot accept,
in what we think
we cannot have,
in who we think
we cannot be.

Salutations from the Sea
    (After Emily Dickinson)

The ocean sent a telegram
Inland to the mountains
Here is my wind
Here is my sea
The smell of fish
Amongst your tall trees,
Roar and foam
To your imagination,
Sea-shells on your mantels.
The mountains send a reply:
Water, water, everywhere,
What a nice surprise,

What starts upward
Must flow down,
The river smiles in gratitude,
I'll see you tomorrow
If the creeks don't rise.
And the birds await what soon
Will rise up from the ground.

The White Curtain

Just there
the white curtain
lifts out from the window
as I pass by,
and I glimpse
oh, that something.
Words are almost
coming from that image.
The suggestion of change,
the good that comes
on a breeze.
So I go back
through the kitchen door
turn around to repeat
and stop at that
one enchanted spot
to listen and feel
it once again.

Moonlight Found Me

Last night the moon
secreted its way
through my window
through a tiny space in the curtain
and fell on the pillow
next to me.
It just happened.
So I put my hand
in that soft light
and caught a little
with open palm.

Light Shining Through Purple Glass

Like golden light shining
through purple glass
high above the trees
clouds and sun
create alchemy
in the fading
light of day.
I've come back
to try and capture
the best of childhood
people and culture
that have passed
symbolized by sun
as the pink cast
over all nature
and this quiet
over the green.
If I go
I will promise to visit
as long as the air
smells this good.

Linda Ann Suddarth was born in Washington, D. C. and grew up in northern Virginia. As an adult she has lived in central and southern Virginia, Georgia, New Jersey, New York City, and Texas. Linda is a collector of landscapes and cultures and so these places are etched in her sensibility and create a lot of questions that play themselves out on sleepless nights and in her writing.

Linda's mother was from a farm in southwest Missouri, and her father was raised from both Washington, D.C. and near Charlottesville, Virginia. As a result of this, she feels that her upbringing was greatly influenced by the 19th more than the 20th century. As an example of this, Linda says that when a teen she just barely escaped being sent to a "finishing school for young ladies." Linda has two children, one resides in the Oakland area, the other resides in New York City and both are very dear and creative people. She has three brothers, all of whom are characters and have resided in Florida. Linda is very influenced by grandparents and a number of powerful and loving great aunts who have played a colorful role in the backdrop of her life.

She has been fortunate to have been taken in-hand throughout her younger life by a number of teachers and mentors, so that along with writing poetry, Linda has always been involved with painting and drawing, theater, literature, folklore, religion, mythology, storytelling, nature, sacred space and mysticism. Poetry made sense in a different way than prose; a deeper way that didn't involve what felt like the narrow confines of logical writing. Reading poetry took Linda through layers of meaning at an early age: the unraveling of puzzles. As she has said, writing poetry is freeing. While sorting through a lot of trouble, Linda started writing poetry obsessively. She wrote around three hundred poems a year for fifteen years. As she has said, a lot of it was not very good, but pieces of it seemed to have a spark. Linda has published forty-five poems in poetry and literary journals, such as *Parabola, Anima, Red River Review, Sojourn* and *Mythopoetry*. Recently she has had some poems published in a Micro-chapbook by Origami Poems Project.

Linda made an unconscious decision a long time ago to stay true to what is freeing. So, in spite of what culture says is important she remains stubborn about being true to creativity and herself. One result of this is that Linda has a B.F.A in Painting and Drawing from Virginia Commonwealth University, an M.A. in Arts and Humanities with an emphasis in Aesthetic Studies from University of Texas at Dallas, and a Ph.D. in Mythological Studies with an emphasis in Depth Psychology from Pacifica Graduate Institute. For her all of these components were part of soul work. Another result of being stubborn is that no matter what is going on she still intends to write, paint, draw, and now enacts the performative in the teaching of Art, English, and Humanities. In teaching Linda finds sneaky ways to focus on the creative process whenever she can.

www.ingramcontent.com/pod-product-compliance
Lightning Source LLC
LaVergne TN
LVHW041517070426
835507LV00012B/1644